THE SMALLEST TREE

One windy afternoon,
the smallest tree in the garden
looked down at the lawn.
There were many, many leaves
lying on the grass at his feet.

"Where did they come from?"
the smallest tree asked himself.
"Are they yours?"
he asked the big tree
standing next to him.

The big tree yawned.
"Yes," she said.

"What will happen,"
the smallest tree asked her,
"when you have no leaves left?"

The big tree yawned again.
"I always lose my leaves
in the autumn," she said.
"When the spring comes,
I put on a new green dress.
In the winter, I sleep,
and I'm very sleepy now."

One morning, when the sun rose,
the smallest tree saw
that the big tree was almost bare.

Quickly, he looked around the garden.
All the other trees were bare, too.

Then he looked down at himself.
He still had all his leaves.
Now the smallest tree
began to feel lonely.
Nobody came out to play
in his shade.
Nobody walked in the garden.

So he played with the wind.
He swished his branches
this way and that.
His leaves rustled
and whispered together.

One night,
there was no wind at all,
but the smallest tree felt
something being sprinkled
all over him.

When dawn came,
he looked down at himself.
His branches were covered with snowflakes
that sparkled in the sunlight.

The smallest tree was very excited!

Suddenly, the front door of the house
was flung open.
A little boy came running out.

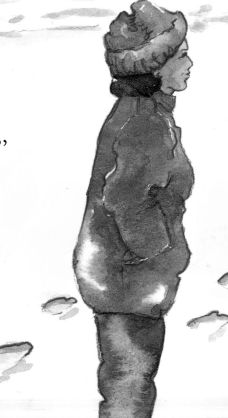

"Hey!" he called.
"Come and see my tree."

"Oh!" said his father.
"I'll get my camera."

"Why does my tree
have all its leaves?"
the boy asked his mother.
"The other trees are bare."

"Your little tree
never loses its leaves,"
said his mother.
"It's an evergreen tree."

When he heard this,
the smallest tree
felt very happy.

He stood very still
and smiled proudly
as they took his photo.